Does Your Organizatio Team Spirit?

Here are 15 building blocks to ensure your team embodies the specific qualities needed for success!

Team spirit is more than just a buzzword, it's the collective attitude and energy that creates cooperation and support. Cultivating this spirit takes skills that can be learned, practiced and perfected. Being on a team means working with others to achieve shared goals through coordinated effort.

In his book, *Your Amazing Itty Bitty™ Legendary Leadership Cultivating Team Spirit,* Ed Nicholls, Jr. reveals essential building blocks that transform a group of individuals into a unified, high-performing team. Featuring the wisdom of legendary basketball coach John Wooden, Ed explores the principles that have shaped championship teams using principles that apply in business, family and friendships.

You'll discover how to:

- Set aside self-importance for the good of the team
- Build a strong foundation of character and values
- Nurture respect and consideration for others
- Become part of something bigger than yourself

If you're ready to build a team based on shared values, mutual respect and a sense of purpose, pick up a copy of this Itty Bitty™ book today!

Your Amazing Itty Bitty™

Legendary Leadership
Cultivating Team Spirit

The 15 Building Blocks of
Championship Caliber Teams

Ed Nicholls Jr., M.Ed.

Published by Itty Bitty™ Publishing
A subsidiary of S&P Productions, Inc.

Printed in the United States of America

Itty Bitty Publishing
311 Main Street, Suite D
El Segundo, CA 90245
(310) 640-8885

ISBN: 978-1-959964-86-5

Dedication

To God who has blessed me and gifted me with the ability to share this message with the world.

To my beautiful wife Stephanie, who is my rock, you changed my life forever ... I LOVE YOU!

To my children, Kaitie, Jay, Ashley, and Celeste, and their families ... you continually inspire me.

To my mom and dad, who taught me everything I needed to know about life.

To Dave for over 50 years of endless friendship and for constantly holding me accountable to me.

To my family, friends, and colleagues who really are the foundation for my successes.

To Suzy, Donna, Pam, and the Itty Bitty team, without you, I'd still be saying *one day...*

To the teachers and students who have allowed me to present this message for 30+ years.

To all who read this and allow the seeds of this message to fill you with hope.

I am grateful for my many blessings!

Stop by our Itty Bitty™ website to find
interesting blog entries regarding
Legendary Leadership at

www.IttyBittyPublishing.com

Or visit **Ed Nicholls Jr.** at

www.legendaryleadershipacademy.com

Table of Contents

Introduction

Your Amazing Itty Bitty™ Legendary Leadership Cultivating Team Spirit book is dedicated to the principle that everyone is part of many teams during the course of their life, but just being on a team is not enough. Being on a team requires individuals to work together to accomplish assigned tasks for the good of the team. Teams are uniquely built and serve various purposes. There are teams like families we're on for life and others are seasonal with team members changing regularly. No matter the type of team you're on, team success requires individuals working together harmoniously. There are specific qualities, characteristics, and skills that can be studied and learned that help individuals and teams achieve true team spirit.

In 1932, a man named John Wooden graduated from Purdue University in Indiana and began a basketball coaching career that would span more than 40 years. He would create a model for leadership and character that outlined the skills required to achieve team spirit. His model defined success as simply, "Do your best." His model included 15 building blocks identifying skills that, when properly cultivated, create championship-caliber teams. Coach Wooden's blocks formed his Pyramid of Success to teach players how to achieve team spirit. He went on to produce 10 NCAA national championship teams.

This book will explain Coach Wooden's building blocks and how each block can be used to cultivate team spirit. Each building block high-lights a legendary leader who used the same principles of team spirit to cultivate exceptionally successful teams. Each block also features a John Wooden coaching tip and a leadership book from the vast library of John Wooden himself. Enjoy this part of your leadership journey!

"A player who makes a team great is better than a great player." **- John R. Wooden, basketball coach, UCLA**

Block 1
Team Spirit

Team spirit is the collective attitude and energy that connects individuals as they develop cooperation and mutual support for team accomplishment. Team spirit is the effort put forth by individuals who learn to disregard their need for self-importance to become a smaller part of something much bigger than themselves.

Cultivating team spirit requires developing skills that can be taught and practiced as follows.

1. A foundation of character and values
2. Strong cooperation and communication
3. Respect and consideration for others
4. Preparation and attention to detail

Team spirit-building skills take time and exercise to develop. Leaders must look for and develop the following:

1. Emphasize effort more than results
2. Concern for team welfare
3. Commitment to excellence
4. Servant leadership mindset
5. Genuine concern for teammates
6. Dedication to crossing the finish line

Role Model: Pat Summitt

Pat Summitt was one of the most successful coaches in women's college basketball. Her leadership style supported her players on and off the court. Her commitment to fundamentals and character were inspired by John Wooden.

- Summitt played women's college basketball in Tennessee, winning a silver medal at the 1976 Olympics for Team USA.
- She won over 1,000 games and eight national championships at the University of Texas. She coached the USA women's basketball team to a gold medal in 1984.

"Teamwork is what makes common people capable of uncommon results."

- Pat Summitt

John Wooden Coaching – Team Spirit

Team spirit is losing oneself for the betterment of the group, eager to sacrifice personal interests for the welfare of all, and being the best part of the team by making those around you better.

From the Wooden Leadership Library

Lessons from the Legends: The Timeless Wisdom of John Wooden and Pat Summitt by Brian Brio

Block 2
Industriousness

The term industriousness refers to hard work, suggesting that team success requires a strong work ethic, persistence, and steady effort. Commitment to hard work requires tedious effort, continual focus, and maintaining a level of discipline when work is especially challenging. Keys to hard work include the following.

1. Hard work is the day-in, day-out grind of accomplishing tasks.
2. Hard work requires attention to detail. Achievement isn't one big accomplishment; it's a series of little steps done well to create team success.
3. Hard work is developing processes and actively preparing for opportunities as they arise.

Team spirit is created through industriousness by showing up for work and getting the job done. There is no substitute for hard work.

1. Industriousness is a cornerstone of team performance, satisfaction, and success.
2. Industriousness creates excitement for the work at hand, leading to group success.

Role Model: Phil Jackson

Phil Jackson is a legendary NBA coach known for his inspirational leadership style. He was deeply influenced by John Wooden. Jackson often referenced Wooden's philosophies in his own coaching approach.

- Phil played for his college basketball team, twice finishing in the Final-Four teams. As a professional player, his New York Knicker-bockers won the 1973 NBA title.
- As an NBA coach, Phil Jackson's Chicago Bulls and Los Angeles Lakers won a combined 11 NBA championships.

"The strength of a team is each team member. The strength of each member is the team."

- Phil Jackson

John Wooden Coaching - Industriousness

You have to be industrious; there is no substitute for hard work. Things worth doing come from hard work and careful planning. Do your best to become the very best you can be.

From the Wooden Leadership Library

Practical Modern Basketball by John Wooden, 1966

Block 3
Friendship

Friendship is an integral part of team success. It enhances team unity and cooperation. Genuine friendship takes two people to build. Over time, it creates a deep foundation of mutual respect and trust, requiring supportive teammates without expectation. In return, the team will be stronger and more successful.

True friendship contributes to overall team success. There are many benefits to cultivating friendships amongst teammates. They include:

1. **Respect** - Fosters collaboration, partnership, and teamwork
2. **Honesty** - Promotes character, reliability, and integrity
3. **Trust** - Creates a solid foundation of cooperation, confidence, and unity
4. **Support -** Builds encouragement and understanding in difficult times, relieves stress between teammates
5. **Growth** - Allows being your absolute best, accountability to the team, and yourself
6. **Happiness** - Creates camaraderie for connection and joy

Role Model: Fred (Mister) Rogers

Fred Rogers was a host, producer, and minister best known for his *Mister Rogers' Neighborhood* television show. He was a friendly, kind, gentle, loving man who educated and comforted children by addressing complex issues with compassion and empathy.

- Mister Rogers was a lifelong advocate of children's television programming and public broadcasting. He welcomed everyone to be part of his neighborhood team.
- He received multiple Emmy Awards, a Lifetime Achievement Award, and the Presidential Medal of Freedom.

"There's no person in the whole world like you. I like you just the way you are."

- Fred Rogers

John Wooden Coaching - Friendship

Every team's success requires a level of friendship. Friendship comes from developing mutual esteem and affection for all. Friendship adds strength to team foundations.

From the Wooden Leadership Library

My Personal Best: Life Lessons from an All-American Journey by John Wooden and Steve Jamison

Block 4
Loyalty

Loyalty is a dedicated commitment to those you lead, care for, and support. Loyalty requires teammates to be reliable, trustworthy, and committed to doing what is right for others, even during the most challenging circumstances. It is essential for building strong relationships, encouraging teamwork, and creating trust and respect in a group or organization.

Great teams are faithfully committed to the following:

1. **Core values** - Holding fast to team principles and the team's moral code, regardless of circumstances
2. **Teamwork** - Prioritizing group success over individual gain and contribution over ambition
3. **Dependability** - Individual reliability in good and bad times
4. **Self-respect** - Remaining steadfast in one's belief and true to the team
5. **Integrity** - Being trustworthy and doing right even when no one is watching
6. **Long-term success** - Building strong, lasting relationships that contribute to personal and professional growth for all

Role Model: Suzy Prudden

Suzy Prudden is an internationally recognized author, publisher, speaker, and wellness expert. She has authored books on health, fitness, weight loss, and personal development. Suzy is a prominent figure in the self-improvement field.

- Suzy co-founded Itty Bitty™ Publishing, inspiring and empowering experts to share their knowledge concisely in short informative books.
- Suzy offers worldwide workshops and seminars to help individuals improve their lives through mindset and wellness strategies.

"Thoughts create reality, so make them positive and powerful."

- Suzy Prudden

John Wooden Coaching - Loyalty

Be loyal to yourself and those dependent upon you. Loyalty is important when situations are difficult. It will produce your best and, in turn, the team's best. Always maintain your self-respect.

From the Wooden Leadership Library

Be Quick-But Don't Hurry: Finding Success in the Teachings of a Lifetime - Andrew Hill and John Wooden

Block 5
Cooperation

Cooperation is a critical component of building a team spirit culture. Cooperation is working together to establish team values, identify common goals, and meet team objectives. Success isn't attained alone. It's the outcome of constant and continuous team effort to gradually produce positive results. The benefits of cooperation include:

1. Nurturing trust, respect, and shared responsibility
2. Promoting harmony, collaboration, and effective problem-solving
3. Enhancing efficiency, strengths, and reducing weaknesses

Leaders only achieve cooperation when team members buy into the process, accept their role, and communicate openly. Focus should be on team success rather than individual acclaim. Cooperation requires:

1. Shared appreciation for others
2. Honest open communication
3. Selflessness over ego
4. An environment of growth and learning
5. A culture of leadership

Role Model: Ruth Bader Ginsburg

Ruth Bader Ginsburg was a lawyer, women's rights advocate, and Supreme Court Justice of the United States. She was only the second woman appointed to the U.S. Supreme Court, where she served 27 years. She was a powerful voice for women's rights, civil rights, and social justice.

- Ruth Bader Ginsburg graduated first in her class at Columbia Law School in 1959.
- Justice Ginsburg served over 40 years as a federal and Supreme Court judge and wrote influential opinions on many cases.

"Fight for the things you care about, but do it in a way that will lead others to join you."
- Ruth Bader Ginsburg

John Wooden Coaching - Cooperation

Cooperation is working together in every way to accomplish a goal. It is expected at every co-working level. Always seek the *best* way rather than insisting on *your* way.

From the Wooden Leadership Library

Life Wisdom from John Wooden, published by Hallmark Books.

Block 6
Enthusiasm

Enthusiasm is passionate enjoyment and excitement for the work you undertake. It provides the energy for perseverance and hard work. It is a cornerstone of team success alongside industriousness. Enthusiasm requires a positive attitude and an eager spirit, which can be contagious when shared with the team. Enthusiasm is built by:

1. Developing passion for the process
2. Creating excitement for activities
3. Motivating and inspiring team members
4. Building resilience in team efforts
5. General optimism and positivity

Leaders must generate enthusiasm and excitement to drive the entire team. Cultivating enthusiasm creates a positive culture both at home and work. It nurtures an environment of encouragement, engagement, and empowerment. Enthusiasm does the following:

1. Gives meaning to work
2. Encourages personal growth
3. Rewards open-mindedness and curiosity
4. Promotes healthy habits and personal care
5. Increases confidence and team production.

Role Model: Theodore Roosevelt

Theodore Roosevelt was the 26th president of the United States, well-known for his energy and enthusiasm. He also supported progressive ideas, environmental conservation efforts, government reform, and was dedicated to making the US great.

- Theodore Roosevelt fought in the Spanish-American War (1898) and led the famous charge up San Juan Hill in Cuba.
- As president, Roosevelt established five national parks and expanded the National Forest Service, preserving millions of acres of wilderness for all to enjoy.

"This country will not be a good place for any of us to live in unless we make it a good place for all of us to live in."

- Theodore Roosevelt

John Wooden Coaching - Enthusiasm

You must enjoy what you're doing; your heart must be in your efforts. Leaders must always generate enthusiasm for team success.

From the Wooden Leadership Library

The Essential Wooden: A Lifetime of Lessons on Leaders and Leadership by John Wooden with Steve Jamison

Block 7
Self-Control

Self-control is the ability to regulate emotions, thoughts, and feelings in pursuit of individual and team goals. Discipline and emotional intelligence are essential to making good decisions, especially under pressure.

Self-control helps as follows:

1. Controlling emotions and behaviors
2. Committing to values and goals
3. Managing distractions
4. Stabilizing effort and productivity
5. Strengthening mental toughness
6. Improving personal relationships

Leaders develop teams using self-control to stay focused on the following aspects of teamwork: mission, vision, and team values. They develop plans to increase self-control in team members by using various methods that may include:

1. Inclusion in strategic planning
2. Developing processes and routines
3. Prioritizing courtesy and thoughtfulness
4. Encouraging accountability to standards
5. Using mistakes as learning opportunities

Role Model: Harriet Tubman

Harriet Tubman was an African-American abolitionist, humanitarian, nurse, and Union Army spy during the American Civil War. She was born into slavery, escaped, and helped other slaves find their way to freedom. In later life, she fought for freedom, women's suffrage, and social justice. She led a life of leadership and courage.

- Harriet Tubman was one of the most famous conductors of the Underground Railroad, helping over 70 enslaved people to freedom.
- Harriet served her country as a nurse, cook, scout, and spy. She led the Combahee raid that freed over 700 enslaved Americans.

"Great dreams begin with a dreamer. You have within you the strength, patience, and passion to reach for the stars and change the world."
- Harriet Tubman

John Wooden Coaching – Self-Control

You cannot function appropriately if your emotions are not under control. Maintaining self-control keeps you focused in the present moment.

From the Wooden Leadership Library

Wooden: A Lifetime of Observations On and Off the Court by John Wooden with Steve Jamison

Block 8
Alertness

Alertness is the ability to be fully aware of and attentive to your surroundings and the activities and events right in front of you. It requires being mentally sharp and quick to respond to changes, opportunities, or threats. The concept of alertness is staying mentally sharp, constantly engaged, and vigilantly focused on responding appropriately to real-time events.

Alertness helps teams to do the following:

1. Avoid complacency
2. Improve decision-making
3. Increase responsiveness
4. Be prepared for anything

It is imperative that leaders remain engaged and connected to the needs of their teams. Staying alert as a leader is crucial to make informed decisions, manage teams effectively, and navigate challenges. To improve alertness, leaders can do the following:

1. Create balanced plans
2. Stay open to new ideas
3. Prioritize good communication
4. Be self-aware and control your emotions
5. Focus on mindfulness and composure

Role Model: Jim Collins

Jim Collins is an author, researcher, and business consultant known for his innovative work in organizational performance and leadership development. Collins is also a speaker and corporate advisor, helping organizations apply his principles to achieve lasting team success.

- Jim Collins authored or co-authored the groundbreaking business and team leadership books, *Built to Last, Good to Great,* and *Great by Choice.*
- He developed the widely used leadership ideas, "Hedgehog Concept," "Level 5 Leadership," and "Flywheel Effect."

"You can accomplish anything in life, provided that you do not mind who gets the credit."
- Jim Collins (Harry Truman)

John Wooden Coaching - Alertness

Be constantly aware and learning. Always seek to improve yourself and the team through awareness, preparation, and adaptability.

From the Wooden Leadership Library

Coach Wooden's Pyramid of Success: Building Blocks for a Better Life by John Wooden and Jay Carty

Block 9
Initiative

Initiative is the ability to make decisions and take action, often under great pressure. It combines knowledge, experience, preparation, and the strength to take the first step toward resolving issues and solving problems. Initiative is a pro-active response to decision-making, taking chances, making mistakes, and viewing failure as a learning experience.

Initiative requires:

1. Decisiveness and determination
2. Courage and resolve
3. Persistence and resilience
4. Creativity and innovation

Great leaders understand that success depends on turning ideas into actionable plans. Eliminating fear can be taught and practiced. It will then be replaced with the confidence to act on your plans. Some steps to build initiative include:

1. Analyzing past decisions
2. Establishing simple goals
3. Exercising decision-making
4. Assigning leadership opportunities

Role Model: Ellen Ochoa

Ellen Ochoa is an American engineer, astronaut, and former director of NASA's Johnson Space Center. She completed a bachelor's degree in physics, and master's degree and PhD in electrical engineering. NASA selected her for astronaut training in 1990.

- Ellen Ochoa was the first Hispanic woman in space aboard Discovery in 1993, and the second woman and first Latina to be named director of the Johnson Space Center (2013).
- Ochoa continues to advocate for women and minorities in the science, technology, engi-neering, and mathematics (STEM) fields.

"Don't be afraid to reach for the stars."

- Ellen Ochoa

John Wooden Coaching - Initiative

You must not be afraid to fail. Failing to act is often the biggest failure of all. Make educated decisions!

From the Wooden Leadership Library

100 Years of Greatness: COACH John Wooden by Matt Fulks

Block 10
Intentness

Intentness is staunch determination, singular focus, and dogged perseverance in the pursuit of team goals. Success is not achieved overnight but requires steady effort, patience, and resilience. Intentness is about staying committed to long-term objectives without getting discouraged by obstacles, distractions, or temporary failures. Following are some key characteristics of intentness.

1. Concentration on small things
2. Strong will to achieve goals
3. Undeterred by setbacks
4. Ongoing consistent effort
5. Short- and long-term vision

Intentness requires faith, perseverance, mental toughness, and strong character. Setbacks and adversity are inevitable, but persistence through challenges with intent will ultimately prevail. The following are characteristics of intentness:

1. Creating clear and detailed plans
2. Providing simple step-by-step processes
3. Encouraging patience and persistence
4. Limiting distractions through structure
5. Developing discipline and accountability

Role Model: Cesar Chavez

César Chávez was a Mexican-American labor leader and civil rights activist who co-founded the United Farm Workers (UFW). He dedicated his life to improving conditions for farm workers through nonviolent resistance, strikes, boycotts, and marches.

- Cesar Chavez co-founded the National Farm Workers Association (NFWA) in 1962, helping it merge to become the United Farm Workers (UFW) in 1966.
- He spent his entire life advocating for fair wages, better working conditions, and union rights for the migrant farmworker labor movement in the United States.

"We cannot seek achievement for ourselves and forget about progress and prosperity for our community."

- Cesar Chavez

John Wooden Coaching - Intentness

Stay the course. When thwarted, work harder and smarter. Concentrate on the objective and reach your goals. Persevere relentlessly!

From the Wooden Leadership Library

Wooden on Leadership by John Wooden and Steve Jamison

Block 11
Condition

Condition is maintaining physical, mental, and emotional health to build a solid foundation for success. Proper conditioning requires individuals to maintain a lifestyle focused on proper nutrition and exercise, while also maintaining a positive mindset, emotional balance, and moral readiness. Maintaining proper condition requires:

1. **Physical** - strength, endurance, flexibility
2. **Mental** - attitude, discipline, resilience
3. **Emotional** - managing stress, composure
4. **Moral** - centered on values, principles

Leaders must constantly reinforce that success is impossible without a solid foundation of physical, mental, and moral readiness. A well-conditioned person is prepared to handle all the challenges of work and life by doing the following:

1. Eat right and exercise regularly
2. Practice mindfulness and manage stress
3. Build discipline through consistent effort
4. Cultivate an attitude of self-awareness

Role Model: Sue Enquist

Sue Enquist is one of the most successful and influential people in college softball history. She spent 27 years at the University of California at Los Angeles, competing as both a player and coach, where she built the UCLA Bruin softball program into a dynasty. As a colleague, Sue was highly influenced by John Wooden's coaching.

- Enquist was the first person to ever win an NCAA softball championship as both a player and a head coach.
- She was an advocate for leadership, team culture, and female empowerment. She led the UCLA Bruins to an unprecedented 11 national championships.

"Anything worthy of your passion should be worthy of your preparation."

- Sue Enquist

John Wooden Coaching - Condition

Ability may get you to the top, but character will keep you there. Constantly condition yourself physically, mentally, emotionally, and morally.

From the Wooden Leadership Library

They Call Me Coach by John Wooden with Jack Tobin

Block 12
Skill

Skill represents a thorough command of the fundamentals required for success in any field of endeavor. True excellence comes from developing and refining individual and team skills through dedicated practice, discipline, and continuous learning. By developing skills, individuals increase their effectiveness and improve their ability to contribute to the team.

Some key aspects of skill are:

1. Mastering fundamentals
2. Performing effectively under pressure
3. Adjusting to varied situations
4. Focusing on accuracy and excellence

Leaders cultivate team success by building a strong foundation of practice, expertise, and continuous improvement. Skill development can be challenging, but it can be accomplished if you:

1. Avoid complacency
2. Stress continual improvement
3. Maintain discipline and accountability
4. Manage frustrations by engaging staff
5. Request feedback and adjust as necessary

Role Model: Tony Dungy

Tony Dungy is a former NFL player, coach, and currently a sports analyst for NBC's Football Night in America. He is known for leadership, integrity, and a calm coaching philosophy.

- Tony Dungy won National Football League Super Bowls 13 and 41 as a player and coach, becoming the first-ever African American coach to win a Super Bowl.
- Tony is actively involved in community outreach, particularly mentorship, education, and social justice. He also gives motivational leadership talks.

"The secret to success is good leadership, and good leadership is all about making the lives of your team members better."

- Tony Dungy

John Wooden Coaching - Skill

Skill is a knowledge of and the ability to properly execute the fundamentals. You must know what you're doing and be able to do it quickly and properly. Be prepared!

From the Wooden Leadership Library

The John Wooden Pyramid of Success by Neville L. Johnson

Block 13
Poise

Poise is the ability of individuals to perform at their very best without being upset by outside influences, criticism, or stress. It involves confidence, grace under pressure, and the ability to remain calm and stay focused regardless of external circumstances. By developing poise, individuals build resilience, improve decision-making, and inspire confidence in others. Some key aspects of poise include:

1. Self-confident in one's training, experience, and ability
2. Maintaining emotional composure during challenges
3. Maintaining grace under pressure when tested in various situations
4. Living authentically and always being true to oneself
5. Being humble by not outdoing others

Those who are comfortable with themselves and trust their preparation will naturally demonstrate poise, an essential quality that leaders develop to make sound decisions and complete responsibilities with certainty and steadiness.

Role Model: Katherine Johnson

Katherine Johnson was an African American mathematician whose groundbreaking calculations were critical to the success of NASA's early space missions. Her proficiency in orbital mechanics helped launch the space program's first orbital trip around Earth in 1962. Her brilliant calculations shaped the future of space travel.

- Katherine Johnson contributed to many space projects including Mercury, Friendship 7, Apollo, Space Shuttle, and Missions to Mars.
- Katherine broke racial and gender barriers in the science and math fields, opening new opportunities for women and minorities in space exploration.

"Like what you do and do your best."
- Katherine Johnson

John Wooden Coaching - Poise

Poise is simply being yourself. Give your total effort to being your very best and being satisfied with your effort. Be at ease in any situation!

From the Wooden Leadership Library

John Wooden's Leadership Game Plan for Life by John Wooden and Steve Jamison

Block 14
Confidence

Confidence is a deep belief in your planning, effort, abilities, and determination. Confidence is the quiet serenity that comes from knowing you have put in the effort to be your best. Confidence requires trust in your preparation, your fellow teammates, and the process of continuous improvement. Key aspects of confidence include:

1. Self-belief in your preparation and skills
2. Fearlessness in succeeding without hesitation or self-doubt
3. Building resilience by recovering from failures with a sense of determination
4. Maintaining composure in challenging situations with singular focus

Confidence is developed through mastery of fundamental skills, consistent practice, and a strong work ethic. Those who prepare thoroughly and put in the necessary effort naturally develop confidence in their abilities. Leaders develop confident teams through:

1. Practice and preparation
2. Learning from mistakes
3. Setting and achieving small goals
4. Support and positivity

Role Model: Eleanor Roosevelt

Eleanor Roosevelt was a human rights activist, diplomat, and the first lady of the United States to her husband, President Franklin D. Roosevelt, from 1933 to 1945. She transformed the role of first lady, becoming a vocal advocate for civil rights, women's rights, and social justice.

- Eleanor Roosevelt served as a U.S. delegate to the United Nations, where she helped create the Universal Declaration of Human Rights in 1948.
- Her leadership and advocacy of civil rights and anti-poverty issues made her one of the most influential women of the 20th century.

"Great minds discuss ideas; average minds discuss events; small minds discuss people."
- Eleanor Roosevelt

John Wooden Coaching - Confidence

You must believe in yourself if you expect others to believe in you. Be confident, but not arrogant. Respect is earned, not given.

From the Wooden Leadership Library

Coach'em Way Up: Five Lessons for Leading the John Wooden Way by Lynn Guerin and Jason Lavin with Jim Eber

Block 15
Competitive Greatness

Competitive greatness is the highest level of achievement. It represents the ability to perform at your best when it matters most, thriving under pressure, and embracing competition with enthusiasm rather than fear. True champions love a challenge; they rise to the occasion in difficult moments. Some key aspects of competitive greatness include:

1. Developing mental toughness
2. Composure under pressure
3. Asserting quiet strength
4. Maintaining a growth mindset
5. Acquiring a true love of competition

By striving for competitive greatness, leaders will maximize their group's potential, inspire team spirit, and achieve lasting success. Some ways to develop competitive greatness are by:

1. Embracing difficulties and challenges
2. Cultivating a tireless work ethic
3. Developing joy for the process of work
4. Engaging, empowering, and encouraging
5. Expecting continuous improvement

Role Model: Vince Lombardi

Vince Lombardi was an American football coach; one of the greatest in National Football League history. His leadership style was known for discipline and dedication, and embodied success and perseverance. His team leadership left a lasting impact on the NFL.

- Vince Lombardi is known for being the head coach of the Green Bay Packers. From 1959-1968, he guided them to five championships, winning the first two Super Bowls.
- Coach Lombardi never had a losing season, was NFL coach of the year twice, and the Super Bowl championship award is named after him, the "Vince Lombardi Trophy."

"Perfection is not attainable, but if we chase perfection, we can catch excellence."
- Vince Lombardi

John Wooden Coaching - Competitive Greatness

Be prepared to perform at your absolute best. You will find that your best is needed every day. Champions love a competitive challenge!

From the Wooden Leadership Library

Coach Wooden One-on-One by John Wooden and Jay Carty

You've finished. Before you go…

Post/Share that you finished this book.

Please star rate this book.

Reviews are solid gold to writers. Please take a few minutes to give us some itty bitty feedback.

ABOUT THE AUTHOR

Ed Nicholls Jr. discovered his passion for leadership at a young age during a visit to New York City with his mother. There he attended an early presentation of Walt Disney's *Great Moments with Mr. Lincoln*, and its powerful portrayal of Abraham Lincoln left a lasting impression on him. Inspired by Lincoln's character and eloquence, Ed developed a deep interest in studying great leaders throughout history.

This passion led him to a distinguished career spanning over forty years in municipal government and law enforcement, where he successfully led numerous teams and organizations. Over time, his leadership studies evolved to focus on key areas such as leadership behavior, strategic planning, and team building. In retirement, Ed founded "The Legendary Leadership Academy," a program designed to inspire and develop leadership skills in individuals, teams, and organizations.

In addition to his dedication to leadership development, Ed has authored three *Itty Bitty* leadership books and created training courses covering topics like leadership growth, strategic planning, and team cohesion. His mission is to empower others to unlock their leadership potential and foster a spirit of excellence.

Ed has been happily married to his wife and partner, Stephanie, for over twenty years. He treasures time spent with his four children, three (and counting) grandchildren, and loved ones. A lifelong sports enthusiast, he enjoys traveling with his wife and staying active through senior softball, pickleball, and golf.

Through it all, Ed remains dedicated to educating, mentoring, and uplifting the human spirit with purpose and vision, continually striving to leave a lasting legacy of hope.

"Team spirit is not about just being on a team; it's about being the best part of the team by making everyone around you better!

- Ed Nicholls Jr.

If you enjoyed this Itty Bitty™ book,
you might also like…

- **Your Amazing Itty Bitty™ Legendary Leadership Academy Handbook** by Ed Nicholls Jr.

- **Your Amazing Itty Bitty™ Legendary Leadership Strategic Planning Guide** by Ed Nicholls Jr.

- **Your Amazing Itty Bitty™ 90-Day Breakthrough** by Scott Lehmann

Or any of the many Amazing Itty Bitty™ books available online at www.ittybittypublishing.com

www.ingramcontent.com/pod-product-compliance
Lightning Source LLC
Chambersburg PA
CBHW071423200326
41520CB00014B/3546